Victoria Rey

Money Magic

**Rituals and Amulets
Wealth & Prosperity
Business, Personal, &
Games of Chance**

© All rights reserved. No part of this book may be reproduced in text or images by any means, without written permission.

© Calli Casa Editorial 2013
© Yhacar Trust, 2024
General Supervision: Bernabé Pérez.
www.2GoodLuck.com
Calli Casa Editorial
Lake Elsinore, CA 92530

INTRODUCTION

UNVEILING THE MAGIC OF MONEY

Have you ever felt like money is a mystery? That financial abundance flows freely to others, while you're left wondering how to attract it into your own life?

Welcome to the world of Money Magic!

This book is here to shatter limiting beliefs and ignite the power within you to create lasting financial security. Forget dry budgeting spreadsheets and restrictive frugality.

Here, we'll explore the surprising truth: abundance is closer than you think, and a little magic can be the key to unlocking it.

We'll delve into the ancient practices of money magic, but with a modern twist. You'll discover how to harness the power of intention, visualization, and practical rituals to transform your financial reality.

This book is not a get-rich-quick scheme; it's a transformative journey that will empower you to:

Shift Your Mindset: Replace scarcity with limitless possibility. Cultivate an abundance mentality that attracts prosperity.

Embrace Rituals: Learn simple, yet powerful, spells and practices to solidify your financial goals and manifest your desires.

Create Money Amulets: Craft personalized talismans infused with your intentions to attract wealth, career success, and abundance.

Practice Gratitude: Discover how appreciating what you already have unlocks the door to receiving even more.

Align with Abundance: Learn to tap into the flow of the Universe and open yourself to receiving financial blessings.

Money Magic is more than just a book; it's an experience. It's about igniting your inner wealth magnet and co-creating a life overflowing with abundance. Are you ready to unlock the magic within? Turn the page and begin your journey to financial freedom!

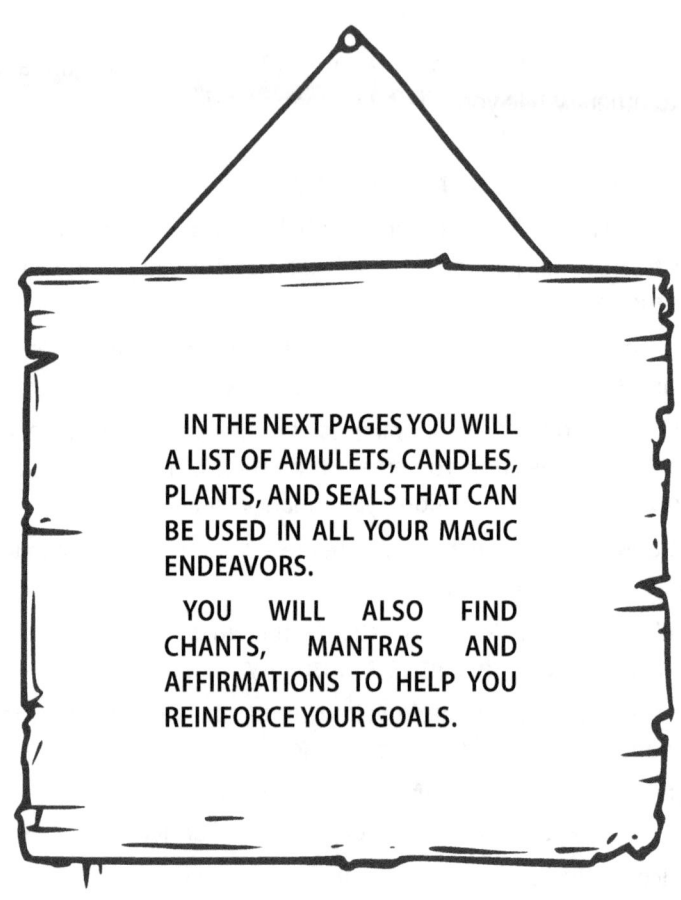

IN THE NEXT PAGES YOU WILL A LIST OF AMULETS, CANDLES, PLANTS, AND SEALS THAT CAN BE USED IN ALL YOUR MAGIC ENDEAVORS.

YOU WILL ALSO FIND CHANTS, MANTRAS AND AFFIRMATIONS TO HELP YOU REINFORCE YOUR GOALS.

AMULETS

You can prepare these amulets by filling a little cloth bag with all the elements included on the recipe. You can sprinkle the amulet with your perfume or with the oils suggested in the formula, or with both. You can add magical seals, one of your hairs, or any other element that makes this amulet completely yours.

Grab a candle, meditate and charge your amulet with the energy of money. While doing this, concentrate on what you want to acomplish (and ditch negative thoughts and negative emotions).

1 FINANCIAL FREEDOM AMULET:

- Crystal: Clear Quartz (amplifies intention and energy)
- Herbs: Bay Leaf (success, prosperity), Spearmint (abundance, growth)
- Oil: Patchouli (attracts wealth), Cinnamon (financial success)
- Other: A small, golden key (symbolic of unlocking financial freedom), a green or gold ribbon (colors of abundance and prosperity)

2 DEBT DESTROYER AMULET:

- Crystal: Citrine (abundance, manifestation)
- Herbs: Rosemary (cleansing, purification), Nettle (represents breaking free)
- Oil: Lemongrass (cleansing negativity), Grapefruit (letting go)
- Other: A small, broken chain (represents breaking the chains of debt), a written list of your debts with a strikethrough symbol (visualize paying them off)

3 PROSPERITY POUCH:

- Fabric: Green or gold (colors of abundance)
- Herbs: A mix of prosperity herbs - Basil (wealth), Cinnamon (success), Clover (luck), Allspice (opportunity)
- Oil: A blend of prosperity oils - Bergamot (abundance), Orange (joy, at-

traction), Ginger (opportunity)

• Other: A small citrine crystal (abundance), a few whole cloves (prosperity symbol), a Chinese coin with a red ribbon (represents wealth)

4. CAREER CATALYST AMULET:

• Crystal: Tiger's Eye (confidence, courage), Carnelian (motivation, action)
• Herbs: Ginkgo Biloba (focus, memory), Sage (wisdom, clarity)
• Oil: Peppermint (mental alertness), Juniper (clearing obstacles)
• Other: A small carnelian pyramid (represents career stability), a resume snippet with your most relevant skills highlighted, a tiny golden star charm (represents reaching for your goals)

5. BUSINESS BOOM AMULET:

• Crystal: Pyrite (abundance, attracting clients), Green Aventurine (growth, new ventures)
• Herbs: Chamomile (calm negotiations), Rue (protection from negativity)
• Oil: Frankincense (success, prosperity), Basil (wealth attraction)
• Other: A miniature handshake charm (represents strong business partnerships), a small golden money bag charm (represents attracting customers and revenue), a business card with a positive affirmation written on the back (e.g., "Clients flock to my business")

6. LUCKY CHARM AMULET:

• Crystal: Amethyst (overall good luck), Malachite (attracts positive circumstances)
• Herbs: Horseshoe clover (luck), Mistletoe (opportunity)
• Oil: Bergamot (abundance), Tangerine (joy, positive energy)
• Other: A small horseshoe charm (traditional luck symbol), a four-leaf clover charm (represents rare good fortune), a personal item imbued with positive memories (a lucky penny you found, a button from a successful interview outfit)

7. ABUNDANCE ANKLET:

• Material: Gold or silver chain (abundance colors)

• Charms: A small cornucopia charm (horn of plenty, symbolizes overflowing abundance), a single pearl (represents wealth and wisdom), a variety of tiny gemstone beads in green (abundance) and gold (prosperity) colors

• Herbs: (Optional) A small pouch filled with dried basil leaves (wealth) sewn onto the inside of the anklet.

• Oil: (Optional) A drop of bergamot oil (abundance) dabbed onto a small piece of cloth and tucked into the pouch with the basil.

8. WINDFALL AMULET:

• Crystal: Blue Apatite (manifestation), Green Aventurine (unexpected opportunities)

• Herbs: Dandelion (represents wishes coming true), Allspice (new opportunities)

• Oil: Tangerine (joy, attracting positive circumstances), Cinnamon (success)

• Other: A small hot air balloon charm (represents windfalls and unexpected gains), a feather (represents lightness and receiving good fortune), a lottery ticket stub from a previous win (to imbue the amulet with luck energy)

9. JOB INTERVIEW AMULET:

• Crystal: Sodalite (confidence, clear communication), Labradorite (transformation, attracting the right opportunity)

• Herbs: Chamomile (calming nerves), Lavender (peace of mind)

• Oil: Peppermint (mental clarity), Grapefruit (confidence)

• Other: A small interview outfit button (connects the amulet to your professional image), a handwritten note with your strengths and accomplishments, a tiny owl charm (represents wisdom and knowledge)

10 NEGOTIATION BOOSTER AMULET:

• Crystal: Amazonite (communication, assertiveness), Pyrite (abundance, attracting what you deserve)
• Herbs: Peppermint (sharp thinking), Nettle (standing your ground)
• Oil: Frankincense (success, confidence), Clary Sage (clear communication)
• Other: A small gavel charm (represents negotiation and reaching agreements), a business card with your desired salary written on the back, a lucky coin you found heads-up (symbolizes success)

11. INVESTMENT INSIGHT AMULET:

• Crystal: Green Aventurine (growth, making wise choices), Amethyst (wisdom, discernment)
• Herbs: Rosemary (clarity, memory), Ginkgo Biloba (focus, sharp thinking)
• Oil: Patchouli (attracting wealth), Frankincense (success, abundance)
• Other: A small compass charm (represents navigating the financial world), a miniature chart with a positive investment symbol, a small pouch containing a written investment goal

12. FRUGAL FOX AMULET:

• Crystal: Citrine (abundance, manifestation), Black Tourmaline (protection from unnecessary spending)
• Herbs: Mint (represents making your money grow), Nettle (standing firm against impulse purchases)
• Oil: Grapefruit (letting go of unnecessary spending), Peppermint (mental clarity for budgeting)
• Other: A small fox charm (the fox is a symbol of resourcefulness and cunning budgeting), a miniature piggy bank charm (represents saving), a written budget plan with a completion date

13. GAMBLER'S GRIMOIRE:

- Materials: A small notebook or leather-bound journal
- Contents: Space to record lucky numbers, dreams that may hold symbolic meaning, personal gambling rituals, affirmations for responsible gambling and setting limits.
- Other: A small pouch containing a single poker chip (represents controlled risk) and a red feather (represents taking a chance).

Disclaimer for Gambler's Grimoire

Please note that gambling should be approached with caution and awareness of the risks involved.

MAGICAL SEALS

Use them on rituals, spells, and amulets, or carry them with you.

You can also put them on any space your want to bring in good vibes, for example, on the door of your house or business, on your altar, or on your sacred space.

FROM THE 6TH AND 7TH BOOKS OF MOSES		

SCHEMHAMPHORAS HOLY SEAL. Used For wealth and for vengeance endeavors.	**SEAL OF ANTIQUELIS.** For wealth, honors, and good health endeavors.	**SEAL OF ORION.** To make wishes come true. To attract success, honor, and respect from others.

SEAL OF POWER. Used to strengthen one's faith, influence others, and to restore one's good health.	**SEAL OF THE SUN OR SEAL OF HONOR AND WEALTH.** Used by those who want to attract all the good things in life.	
	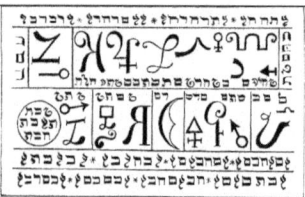	
SEAL OF FORTUNE. To draw blessings and success in business, family, and personal affairs.	**SEAL OF GREAT GENERATION.** To draw honor, wealth, and to obtain promotions.	

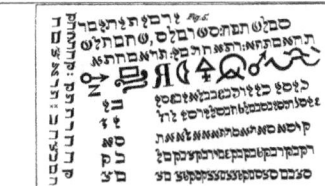	
SEAL OF LONG LIFE. This seal is used by those seeking to have a full, long, and happy life.	**SEAL OF MERCURY.** Used for communication accuracy, to assure wealth, to unearth treasures, and to master alchemy and chemistry.

FROM THE SEALS OF SOLOMON

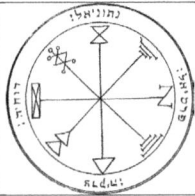			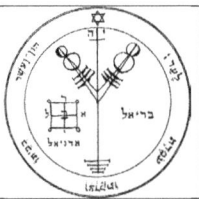
1. To attract wealth and prosperity in business.	**2.** To attract riches, honors, and peace of mind.	**3.** Protection from evil spirits that may cause negative conditions.	**4.** To gain and retain wealth and honors. Combine with #2.

FROM THE SEALS OF THE SPIRITS

		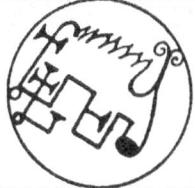	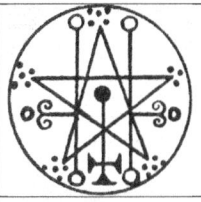
BUNE OR BIMÉ #26. Grants the ability to use words with elegance and acuity. Brings in wealth and prosperity.	**FORAS #31.** Teaches knowledge on stones, and plants, as wll as logic. Helps recover lost things and promotes wealth and wisdom.	**AMY, OR AVNAS #58.** Helps uncover hidden treasures. Promotes wealth and good fortune. Enlightens in astrology issues.	**ASTAROTH #29.** Reveals the future through visions and dreams. Helps the sorcerer to uncover the unknown.

FROM DIFFERENT SOURCES			
VOODOO VEVE	**HEX SIGNS**	**SAGE PF THE PYRAMIDS**	**JAPANESE**
PAY ME NOW. To collect any money or promises owed to the possessor.	**SUCCESS, WEALTH, AND PROSPERITY.** Put this sign on your house or on your business to bless and prosper the place.	**GOETIC CIRCLE.** This circle should be worn on the clothes while casting spells, to make all his desires come to pass, and his or her magic to be more effective.	**THE KEYS OF THE GRANARY.** Japanese. Worn for love, wealth, and happiness.

CHINESE	
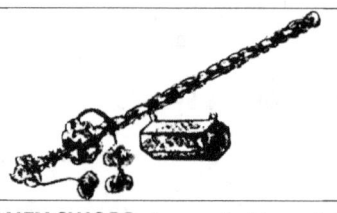	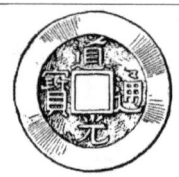
THE MONEY SWORD. Suspended from right to left above the head of the bed. All powerful protection against ill-luck, and evil spirits. Also attracts cash.	**COINS.** Used to bring in wealth, positive energies, and prosperity.

TIBETAN	HINDU	
LUCKY DIAGRAM. Longevity and Well being.	**LOTUS.** Good luck, good fortune, and beauty.	**THE CONCH SHELL.** The bringer of wealth, oratory teacher, and aid in any type of learning.

CANDLES FOR WEALTH AND PROSPERITY MEDITATION:

Candle meditations are a tool to support your financial goals. Combine them with financial planning and taking action for true abundance.

Here's a list of colored candles, their symbolic associations, and a dressing formula to use them in your wealth and prosperity meditations:

Gold	Overall abundance, prosperity, success
Green	Growth, new opportunities, attracting wealth
Yellow	Confidence, optimism, attracting positive circumstances
White	Purity, new beginnings, clearing financial blockages
Orange	Joy, creativity, attracting abundance
Brown	Stability, security, grounding financial goals
Purple	Ambition, luxury, achieving financial goals
Indigo	Intuition, wisdom, making sound financial decisions
Teal	Abundance at sea (good for investments, business ventures)
Pink	Love, appreciation, self-worth (important for a healthy relationship with money)
Red	Passion, motivation, taking action towards financial goals
Black	Banishing negativity, protection from financial loss
Silver	Success in business ventures, attracting clientele

CANDLE DRESSING FORMULA:

1. CLEANSE YOUR SPACE: Before dressing your candle, cleanse your meditation space with sage smoke or by sprinkling salt water (visualize negative energy being carried away).

2. CHOOSE YOUR CANDLE: Select a candle color that resonates with your current financial intention (refer to the table above for guidance).

3. ANOINT THE CANDLE: Using a natural oil that complements your intention (e.g., patchouli oil for attracting wealth, frankincense oil for success), lightly anoint the candle from wick to base in a circular motion.

4. CARVE INTENTIONS (OPTIONAL): If you wish, you can carve symbols or words that represent your financial goals into the candle (e.g., dollar sign, abundance).

5. DRESS WITH HERBS (Optional): Sprinkle a few dried herbs associated with wealth and prosperity around the base of the candle (refer to the previous list of plants for suggestions).

6. LIGHT THE CANDLE: Focus on your breath and light the candle. Visualize the flame burning away any negativity or limitations surrounding your finances.

7. MEDITATE: AS THE candle burns, use visualization techniques or affirmations to solidify your wealth intentions. See yourself achieving your financial goals and feeling abundant.

8. EXTINGUISH THE CANDLE: When your meditation is complete, extinguish the flame with a snuffer cap (prevents smoke and wick damage).

SAFETY NOTE: NEVER LEAVE a burning candle unattended.

HERBS WITH MONEY DRAWING ENERGY

	BASIL: A CULINARY HERB associated with attracting wealth and prosperity.
	CINNAMON: A WARMING SPICE used to symbolize financial flow and success.
	CLOVER (FOUR-LEAF): A RARE variant of the clover plant, considered a lucky charm that attracts good fortune, including financial blessings.
	FERN: BELIEVED TO ATTRACT wealth and unexpected windfalls.
	ALLSPICE: REPRESENTS NEW OPPORTUNITIES and the expansion of wealth.
	GINGER: A ROOT SYMBOLIZING growth and attracting fresh streams of income.
	JASMINE: KNOWN FOR ITS association with good luck, abundance, and prosperity.
	MINT (SPEARMINT OR PEPPERMINT): Represents growth, abundance, and new financial beginnings.
	OAK: A SYMBOL OF strength, stability, and manifesting long-term financial security.
	ORANGE: THE FRUIT AND tree are linked to joy, abundance, and attracting success.
	PATCHOULI: AN EARTHY HERB with a musky scent, used in spells to attract wealth and prosperity.
	ROSEMARY: OFTEN USED FOR purification and cleansing rituals, preparing the way for financial blessings to flow freely.
	SAGE: ASSOCIATED WITH WISDOM, good decision-making, and attracting financial security.

CHANTS

Use these changes when making your amulets; when casting spells; in magical ceremonies or any time you need to reconnect with your inner prosperity.

1. FINANCIAL FREEDOM CHANT:

Clear quartz shines bright, my will takes flight, I break free from burdens, with all my might. Abundance flows, my future aglow, Financial freedom, to me it shall grow.

2. DEBT DESTROYER CHANT:

Citrine's light, cuts through the night, Debt chains I sever, with focused might. Rosemary cleanses, with purpose it means, Debt disappears, a brand new scene.

3. PROSPERITY CHANT:

Green and gold hold, a story untold, Herbs of abundance, in my pouch unfold. Oils of attraction, bring forth satisfaction, Prosperity beckons, with joyous reaction.

4. CAREER CATALYST CHANT:

Tiger's eye gleaming, my courage is beaming, Carnelian fire, fuels my desire. Focus and clarity, pave the way clearly, Career success, awaits me dearly.

5. BUSINESS BOOM CHANT:

Pyrite gleams bright, attracting with might, Clients come calling, bathed in golden light. Frankincense graces, success embraces, Business booms onward, in prosperous spaces.

6. LUCKY CHARM CHANT:

Amethyst shimmers, good fortune it glimmers, Malachite's green, keeps my path clean. Horseshoe's protection, brings joyful direction, Luck overflows, with endless affection.

7. ABUNDANCE CHANT

(Can be chanted silently as a walking meditation):

With each step I take, abundance I wake, Golden chain gleaming, prosperity dreaming. Tiny gems whisper, secrets they quiver, Wealth flows freely, forever and ever.

8. WINDFALL CHANT:

Blue apatite's spark, ignites a lucky lark, Aventurine's green, unexpected scenes. Feathers of lightness, bring moments of brightness, Windfall arrives, filling my life with light.

9. JOB INTERVIEW CHANT:

Sodalite whispers, calming my jitters, Labradorite's glow, helps my confidence flow. Chamomile soothes, anxieties it smoothes, Interview aced, future unfolds.

10. NEGOTIATION BOOSTER CHANT:

Amazonite sings, my voice clearly rings, Pyrite shines bold, worth I shall hold. Peppermint sparks, sharpens my remarks, Agreements I capture, leaving nothing to rapture.

11. INVESTMENT INSIGHT CHANT:

Green Aventurine gleams, wise choices it beams, Amethyst's wisdom, protects from a chasm. Rosemary recalls, knowledge through walls, Ginkgo empowers, for prosperous hours.

12. FRUGAL FOX CHANT:

Citrine's light, attracts what is right, Black Tourmaline shields, from unnecessary fields. Mint wisely grows, my money it knows, Nettle stands strong, against spending songs.

13. GAMBLER'S CHANT:

Something to think about: Approach gambling with caution and awareness.

Red feather dares, controlled risk it shares, Poker chip gleams, setting my limits and means. Grimoire unfolds, stories untold, Luck I may find, but responsibility I hold.

MANTRAS

Here is a list of mantras you can repeat when you wake up, before going to sleep, or any time of the day or night you need to ditch worry and reclaim your connection to the abundance of the Universe.

	1. PROSPERITY SURROUNDS ME. I am open to receive. (Short and rhythmic for easy repetition)
	2. WEALTH FLOWS FREELY. I am a magnet, attracting abundance. (Focuses on the flow of money)
	3. GRATITUDE UNLOCKS ABUNDANCE. I am thankful for all I have. (Connects gratitude with financial gain)
	4. DEBT DISSOLVES, REPLACED by prosperity. I am financially free. (Powerful visualization for debt repayment)
	5. EVERY EXPENSE IS an investment. My money grows with wisdom. (Shifts perspective on spending)
	6. WISE CHOICES LEAD to wealth. I make sound financial decisions. (Focuses on responsible money management)
	7. UNEXPECTED WINDFALLS SURPRISE me. The Universe provides. (Attracts unexpected financial gains)
	8. ABUNDANCE IS MY birthright. I claim my financial security. (Empowering statement of worthiness)
	9. MY INCOME EXPANDS with each passing day. Prosperity grows within me. (Focuses on income growth)
	10. LIMITED BELIEFS ARE released. I am limitless in my financial potential. (Breaks down mental barriers)
	11. CHALLENGES ARE STEPPING stones. I overcome obstacles for financial success. (Transforms challenges into opportunities)
	12. EVERY ACTION LEADS to abundance. I take inspired steps towards my goals. (Connects action with financial growth)
	13. I AM WORTHY and deserving. Wealth flows to me effortlessly. (Simple and positive self-affirmation)

WEALTH AFFIRMATIONS

Write these affirmations on a piece of paper and put it where you can see it every time you are doing your chores.

CHECK	REPEAT
	1. I AM A magnet for abundance. Prosperity flows to me freely and effortlessly.
	2. MY INCOME IS constantly expanding. I am worthy of financial success.
	3. I RELEASE LIMITING beliefs about money and embrace my limitless potential.
	4. GRATITUDE FILLS MY heart. I am surrounded by financial blessings.
	5. EVERY CHALLENGE IS an opportunity for growth and financial abundance.
	6. I MAKE WISE financial decisions with confidence and clarity.
	7. DEBT HAS NO hold on me. I am financially free and empowered.
	8. ABUNDANCE IS MY birthright. I deserve to live a prosperous life.
	9. UNEXPECTED OPPORTUNITIES FOR wealth come to me easily and often.
	10. MY MONEY GROWS and multiplies with each passing day.
	11. I AM ALIGNED with the Universe's flow of abundance. My needs are always met.
	12. FINANCIAL SECURITY AND peace of mind are mine. I am grateful.
	13. I AM A powerful creator. I attract wealth with my thoughts, intentions, and actions.

DEBT REPAYMENT RITUALS: BREAKING FREE FINANCIALLY

Debt can feel like a heavy burden, weighing you down and hindering your financial freedom. Money magic offers symbolic rituals to empower you on your debt-free journey. These rituals work best when combined with a solid debt repayment plan, but they can add a powerful emotional and energetic boost to your efforts. Here are a few ideas:

1. THE BURNING DEBT LETTER:

• Materials: A piece of paper, a pen, a fireproof bowl or cauldron (optional).

• Instructions: Write down a detailed list of all your debts, including the creditor name, amount owed, and minimum payment. Express your gratitude to the debt for serving its purpose (e.g., helping you buy a car). Declare your intention to be free from this debt and visualize yourself living a debt-free life. Fold the paper and light it safely in a fireproof bowl (if outdoors) or visualize it burning in your mind's eye. As the paper burns (or you visualize it burning), see your debt dissolving with it.

2. THE DEBT JAR RELEASE RITUAL:

• Materials: A clear jar with a lid, small pieces of paper, pens in different colors (optional).

• Instructions: For each debt you have, write down the amount owed and the creditor's name on a separate piece of paper. Use different colored pens to differentiate between debts (optional). Fold the papers and place them in the jar. As you add each piece, visualize yourself making a successful debt payment. Shake the jar vigorously, symbolizing the shaking loose of your debt burden. Close the jar tightly and place it somewhere you'll see it daily as a reminder of your commitment to debt repayment. Once a debt is paid off, remove the corresponding paper from the jar and celebrate your accomplishment!

3. THE COIN REPAYMENT RITUAL:

• Materials: A jar, coins of various denominations (enough to represent a small portion of your debt), a permanent marker.

• Instructions: Write the amount of a specific debt you want to tackle on the jar. For each debt payment you make, place a coin in the jar, visualizing the debt shrinking with each deposit. The sound of the coins clinking can be a satisfying reminder of your progress. Once the jar is full, use the collected coins towards your next debt payment, imbuing them with the positive energy of your ritual.

4. THE MONEY TREE ABUNDANCE SWITCH:

• Materials: A healthy houseplant (consider a money plant!), green ribbon, small pieces of paper.

• Instructions: Write down on each piece of paper a specific amount you intend to pay towards your debt. Tie these papers to the branches of your money plant with green ribbon (symbolizing growth and abundance). As you make debt payments, remove the corresponding paper from the plant and visualize your debt burden decreasing. Caring for your money plant becomes a metaphor for nurturing your financial well-being.

5. THE DEBT-CRUSHING AFFIRMATION BATH:

• Materials: Bathwater, sea salt (optional), essential oil blend for abundance or prosperity (optional), a small pouch (optional).

• Instructions: Draw a warm bath and add sea salt or a few drops of an essential oil blend (if desired). As you soak, visualize yourself surrounded by white light, symbolizing financial freedom. Repeat positive affirmations like "I am worthy of financial abundance," "Debt has no hold on me," or "I am breaking free financially." You can write these affirmations on a piece of paper and place them in a small pouch worn around your neck during the bath for an extra touch.

Something to think about:, these rituals are meant to be a symbolic and emotional boost alongside your concrete debt repayment plan. Be consistent with your efforts, and harness the power of intention to break free from debt and create a financially secure future.

DECLUTTER FOR ABUNDANCE: CREATING SPACE FOR FINANCIAL FLOW

Have you ever noticed how a cluttered physical space can feel overwhelming and stagnant? The same principle applies to your finances. Holding onto unnecessary possessions can create energetic blockages that hinder the flow of abundance. Decluttering for abundance is not just about getting rid of stuff; it's about creating space for financial growth and prosperity. Here's how to get started:

1. SHIFT YOUR MINDSET:

Before you begin, approach decluttering with the intention of creating space for new opportunities, not just getting rid of things. Visualize the abundance you desire flowing into your life as you clear physical clutter.

2. START SMALL AND SPECIFIC:

Don't overwhelm yourself by tackling your entire home at once. Choose a specific area, like a drawer, shelf, or closet, and focus on decluttering that space. This will give you a sense of accomplishment and motivate you to continue.

3. ASK YOURSELF KEY QUESTIONS:

As you go through your belongings, ask yourself these questions for each item:

- Does this spark joy? (Inspired by the KonMari method)
- Have I used this in the past year?
- Would I buy this again today?
- Does this item serve a purpose, or is it just taking up space?

4. CATEGORIZE AND DISPOSE:

Once you've sorted through your belongings, categorize them into four piles: keep, sell, donate, or discard. Here are some tips for each category:

- Keep: Only keep items that bring you joy, serve a purpose, or hold sentimental value.

• Sell: Consider online marketplaces or consignment shops for gently used items you no longer need. This can even generate some extra income.

• Donate: Give unwanted items in good condition to charity, helping others while decluttering your space.

• Discard: Dispose of broken, unusable, or expired items responsibly.

5. DECLUTTER YOUR FINANCES:

Decluttering doesn't stop with physical objects. Review your bank statements and cancel unused subscriptions or memberships. Unsubscribe from unnecessary email lists that contribute to digital clutter. This can free up extra money and mental space.

6. EMBRACE THE ABUNDANCE MINDSET:

As you declutter, visualize the abundance that will flow into the newly created space. This could be financial wealth, new opportunities, or simply a sense of peace and clarity.

Something to think about: Decluttering for abundance is a continuous process. Schedule regular decluttering sessions to maintain a clear and inviting space, both physically and financially. As you release what no longer serves you, you open yourself up to receiving the abundance you deserve.

FENG SHUI FOR WEALTH: ATTRACTING ABUNDANCE WITH SPATIAL HARMONY

Feng Shui, the ancient Chinese practice of arranging elements to create harmonious flow, can be a powerful tool for attracting wealth and prosperity. Here are some basic principles to optimize your living space for financial abundance:

1. THE WEALTH CORNER:

The southeast sector of your home is considered the wealth corner according to the Bagua map, a tool used in Feng Shui. Activate this area to enhance your money luck.

• Colors: Decorate this area with wealth-activating colors like green (growth), purple (prosperity), or gold (abundance).

• Symbols: Place symbols of wealth and abundance in the wealth corner, such as a money plant, a wealth bowl filled with coins or gemstones, or a ship filled with treasure (symbolic of receiving wealth).

• Water Features: A small tabletop fountain or a healthy fish tank can represent the flow of wealth. However, avoid stagnant water, which can symbolize blocked finances.

2. THE FRONT DOOR: THE GATEWAY TO OPPORTUNITY

Your front door is the entry point for energy into your home, including financial opportunities.

• Keep it Clean and Inviting: Maintain a clean and clutter-free entryway. A cluttered entryway can block the flow of positive energy.

• Doormat: Place a welcoming doormat in front of your door. Choose a rectangular shaped mat, as rounded shapes symbolize money flowing out.

• Color: Painting your front door a prosperous color like red (vibrant energy) or gold (abundance) can enhance your curb appeal and symbolically invite wealth in.

3. THE LIVING ROOM: ABUNDANCE AND PROSPERITY

The living room is a central gathering space, and Feng Shui principles here can promote financial well-being.

• Command Position: Arrange your furniture so the main seating area (where you entertain guests) is in a commanding position, facing the door. This position symbolizes control and security over your finances.

• Declutter and Maintain Open Space: Avoid overcrowding your living room with furniture. Create a sense of spaciousness to allow the flow of positive chi (energy).

• Affirmations and Visualizations: Display positive affirmations or inspiring artwork related to wealth and abundance in your living room.

4. THE KITCHEN: SOURCE OF NOURISHMENT AND WEALTH

The kitchen is associated with abundance and sustenance. Here's how to optimize its energy for financial flow:

• Keep it Clean and Orderly: Maintain a clean and organized kitchen. A cluttered kitchen can lead to stagnant energy and hinder financial well-being.

• The Stove: A functional stove symbolizes a steady income. If your stove is broken or not in use, consider repairing or replacing it.

• Invite Abundance: Place a bowl of fresh fruit on your counter, symbolizing abundance and attracting prosperous energy.

5. THE BEDROOM: REST AND RECHARGE

Your bedroom is a place for rest and rejuvenation, which is essential for pursuing financial goals.

• Electronics Away: Avoid keeping electronics like TVs or laptops in your bedroom. These disrupt sleep and can introduce chaotic energy that hinders financial focus.

• Mirrored Nightstands (Optional): While some Feng Shui practitioners advise against mirrored nightstands, others believe they can symbolically double your wealth.

Something to think about: Feng Shui is not a quick fix, but a way to create a harmonious and supportive environment for your financial goals. Combine these principles with sound financial planning and effort to cultivate lasting financial abundance.

CHARITY AND ABUNDANCE: THE POWER OF GIVING

The concept of giving back to those in need might seem counterintuitive on the path to financial abundance. However, the idea behind charity and abundance is rooted in the principle of flow. Just as stagnant water becomes murky and unusable, stagnant wealth can feel restrictive. Here's how incorporating charity into your money magic practice can unlock a deeper level of abundance:

1. THE LAW OF ATTRACTION:

The Law of Attraction posits that like attracts like. By giving generously, you put out positive energy of abundance into the Universe. This act of giving opens you up to receiving abundance in return, not just financially, but in other aspects of life as well.

2. THE ABUNDANCE MINDSET:

Charity fosters an abundance mindset. When you focus on sharing your resources, it reinforces the belief that you have enough, and more will come. It shifts your perspective from scarcity to a place of trust and generosity, which can be a powerful attractor for abundance.

3. GRATITUDE THROUGH GIVING:

The act of giving cultivates gratitude for what you already have. This appreciation opens you up to receiving even more blessings. Focusing on the positive impact your donation creates fosters a sense of abundance beyond just material possessions.

4. KARMA AND THE CYCLE OF GIVING:

Many cultures believe in the concept of karma, where good deeds are returned in kind. By giving to charity, you're contributing to a positive cycle of giving and receiving. This doesn't mean you'll get a direct financial return for every donation, but it reinforces the idea of abundance flowing through your life.

5. THE JOY OF GIVING:

Giving back to causes you care about can bring immense joy and satisfaction. This positive emotion elevates your overall well-being and can attract more abundance into your life.

INTEGRATING CHARITY INTO YOUR MONEY MAGIC:

• Set Aside a Giving Percentage: Allocate a specific percentage of your income to charity, just like you would a bill. This creates a habit of giving and reinforces the idea that you have enough to share.

• Research Charities: Choose charities that resonate with your values and causes you're passionate about. This makes the act of giving more meaningful and impactful.

• Make Giving a Ritual: Incorporate giving into your money magic rituals. Light a candle with the intention of abundance, then donate a set amount to your chosen charity. Visualize the positive impact your donation creates.

• Gratitude for What You Have: After a successful financial milestone, express your gratitude by giving to charity. This reinforces the abundance mindset and creates a positive cycle of receiving and giving.

Something to think about: charity is not about feeling obligated or giving from a place of lack. It's about aligning yourself with the flow of abundance and contributing to a more positive world. By giving back, you open yourself up to receiving more abundance in all aspects of your life.

MONEY, MYTHOLOGY AND ƒOKLORE

Money mythology and folklore are rich tapestries woven from cultural beliefs, explanations for prosperity, and even warnings about the dangers of wealth. Here's a glimpse into some fascinating stories and traditions:

1. THE LEPRECHAUN'S POT of Gold (Irish Folklore): These mischievous creatures are said to hide a pot of gold at the end of a rainbow. While not a literal representation of wealth, it symbolizes the potential for unexpected windfalls and the elusive nature of riches.

2. THE MIDAS MYTH (Greek Mythology): King Midas wished for everything he touched to turn to gold. His joy turned to horror as even his food and daughter became gold. This myth serves as a cautionary tale about the dangers of greed and the importance of appreciating what cannot be bought.

3. THE COIN IN the New Moon Ritual (Many Cultures): In various cultures, there's a tradition of showing a coin to the new moon for good luck and prosperity. The new moon symbolizes new beginnings, and the coin represents attracting wealth during this growth phase.

4. THE GIVING TREE (Shel Silverstein): This children's book tells the story of a selfless tree that gives everything it has to a boy. While the boy becomes greedy and demanding, the tree withers away. This story serves as a reminder of the importance of balance and not letting greed overshadow generosity.

5. THE GRATITUDE STONE (Various Cultures): In some cultures, people carry smooth stones as a reminder to be grateful for their blessings, including financial security. Holding the stone and expressing gratitude is believed to attract more abundance.

6. THE MONEY-LENDING MERMAID (Japanese Folktale): This tale tells the story of a fisherman who helps a mermaid. In return, she grants him a wish, and he foolishly wishes for an endless pot of gold. The gold overflows and buries him, highlighting the importance of measured desires and responsible handling of wealth.

7. THE LUCKY RED Envelope (Chinese New Year Tradition): Red envelopes filled with money are given during Chinese New Year, symbolizing good luck and prosperity for the recipient. It signifies the importance of sharing wealth and blessings with loved ones.

8. BANSHEE WARNINGS (IRISH Folklore): The banshee, a wailing spirit, is said to herald the death of a family member. However, in some variations, her cries can also warn of impending financial hardship. This folklore highlights the unpredictable nature of wealth and the importance of responsible financial planning.

Something to think about: money mythology and folklore are not just entertaining stories; they offer valuable lessons about wealth, greed, gratitude, and the importance of a balanced approach to financial well-being. As you explore these traditions, you might find inspiration and guidance for your own money magic practice.

DEITIES THAT REPRESENT WEALTH, GOOD FORTUNE AND PROSPERITY

XI WANGMU (XIWANGMU) FROM CHINESE MYTHOLOGY.

She is also known as the Queen Mother of the West or the Golden Mother of the West. Xi Wangmu is associated with:

• Immortality and Longevity: She is said to reside in a heavenly peach orchard that grants immortality to those who eat the peaches.

• Fertility: She is associated with the birth and nurturing of life.

• Abundance: She is seen as a ruler of the West, which was associated with the harvest and abundance in Chinese culture.

• Good Life: By extension of the above, she is connected with blessings for a prosperous and fulfilling life.

BENZAITEN (BENTEN):

• Origin: East Asian Buddhist goddess (technically a Dharmapala, "Dharma protector") who originated mainly from the Hindu Indian Saraswati, goddess of speech, the arts, and learning.

• Domains:

+ Wealth and Prosperity

+Knowledge and Wisdom

+Art, Music, and Creativity

+Water and Rivers

+ Luck and Fortune

• Depiction: Often depicted holding a biwa (a traditional Japanese lute) and sometimes accompanied by a white snake, which serves as her messenger.

• Significance: Benzaiten is one of the Seven Lucky Gods in Japan, revered for bringing not just material wealth but also good fortune in creative pursuits, knowledge, and eloquence. She is also associated with water, symbolizing the flow of abundance and the cleansing power of knowledge.

HINDUISM:

• Lakshmi: The most prominent deity associated with wealth and prosperity in Hinduism.

• Kubera: The God of wealth and the lord of yakshas (nature spirits).

GREEK MYTHOLOGY:

• Plutus: The Greek god of wealth, associated with agriculture and commerce.

• Tyche: The Greek goddess of fortune and prosperity, associated with luck, chance, and unexpected windfalls.

ROMAN MYTHOLOGY:

• Fortuna: The Roman goddess of fortune, luck, and prosperity.

Egyptian Mythology:

• Bastet: The cat goddess associated with protection, good health, and prosperity.

NORSE MYTHOLOGY:

• Gefion: The Norse goddess associated with prosperity, particularly agricultural wealth and fertility of the land.

THAI FOLK RELIGION:

• Nang Kwak: The Thai goddess of wealth, fortune, and good luck.

• Phosop: Another Thai deity associated with wealth and prosperity, particularly for business owners and merchants.

OTHER CULTURES:

• Inti (Inca Empire): The sun god, also associated with wealth and prosperity.

• Ebisu (Japan): The god of good fortune, business, and commerce.

• Xochipilli (Aztec Mythology): The god of wealth, merchants, games, beauty, and dance.

CREATING A MONEY ALTAR: A SACRED SPACE FOR ABUNDANCE

Your money altar is a dedicated space that serves as a physical manifestation of your financial goals and intentions. It's a place to focus your energy, perform rituals, and connect with the flow of abundance. Here's how to create a powerful money altar:

1. CHOOSE THE RIGHT LOCATION:

Select a quiet and clutter-free area in your home where you won't be disturbed. It should be a space that inspires feelings of peace and focus.

2. SELECT A BASE:

Use a decorative table, tray, or even a specific section of your shelf as the base for your altar. Consider the materials – wood symbolizes growth, while metal represents stability. Choose what resonates with your financial goals.

3. THE ALTAR CLOTH:

Cover your base with a cloth that represents abundance or prosperity. Green or gold are popular choices, but ultimately, choose a color that evokes positive financial feelings for you.

4. SYMBOLS OF WEALTH AND ABUNDANCE:

- Coins and Currency: Place a variety of coins or bills (real or symbolic) on your altar. Foreign currency can symbolize attracting wealth from diverse sources.
- Crystals for Money Magic: Select crystals associated with abundance, such as citrine (attracts wealth), pyrite (abundance and prosperity), or aventurine (new opportunities).
- Figures of Prosperity: Statues or figurines of deities associated with wealth (e.g., Lakshmi in Hinduism, Fortuna in Roman mythology) or lucky symbols like horseshoes or four-leaf clovers can be powerful additions.

5. PERSONALIZE YOUR ALTAR:

• Affirmation Cards: Place cards with positive financial affirmations on your altar to reinforce your beliefs.

• Sigils or Money Mantras: Create or write down sigils (symbolic representations) of your financial goals or money mantras to keep your focus clear.

• Prosperity Herbs: Dried herbs associated with wealth, like basil, cinnamon, or mint, can add a touch of nature's abundance.

• Lucky Charms: Include your personal lucky charms or objects that inspire feelings of wealth and success.

6. DEDICATION AND ACTIVATION:

Once your altar is complete, cleanse the space with sage smoke or visualization. Light a candle to symbolize your intentions and dedicate your altar to attracting abundance.

7. MAINTAINING YOUR ALTAR:

Regularly dust and cleanse your altar to maintain its energetic potency. Spend time near your altar for meditation, visualization, or simply to connect with your financial goals.

Something to think about: your money altar is a personal and dynamic space. Allow your intuition to guide you as you create and maintain it. As you focus your energy on this sacred space, you'll be strengthening your intentions and attracting the financial abundance you deserve.

MOON MAGIC FOR MONEY: HARNESSING LUNAR ENERGIES FOR ABUNDANCE

The moon, with its ever-changing phases, has captivated humanity for centuries. In money magic, the moon's influence is harnessed to attract wealth, prosperity, and financial success. Here's how you can utilize the lunar cycle to empower your financial goals:

NEW MOON:

- Energy: Beginnings, new opportunities, setting intentions.
- Money Magic: This is a potent time for planting seeds of wealth. Write down your financial goals and wishes with clear intention. Carry these intentions with you throughout the lunar cycle.
- Ritual Ideas: Create a vision board representing your financial desires. Light a white candle to symbolize new beginnings and illuminate your path to abundance.

WAXING MOON (CRESCENT TO GIBBOUS):

- Energy: Growth, expansion, taking action.
- Money Magic: Focus on taking concrete steps towards your financial goals. Research investment opportunities, network with people in your field, or start a side hustle.
- Ritual Ideas: Perform a money sigil ritual. Create a sigil (symbolic representation) of your financial desires and charge it with lunar energy under the waxing moon.

FULL MOON:

- Energy: Abundance, culmination, peak energy.
- Money Magic: Celebrate your progress and express gratitude for any financial blessings you've received. This is also a powerful time for abundance rituals.
- Ritual Ideas: Perform a Full Moon Money Bath. Draw a bath with water infused with herbs associated with wealth (e.g., basil, cinnamon) and visua-

lize abundance flowing into your life. Count your blessings (money in your wallet, savings account, etc.) while basking in the full moon's light.

WANING MOON (GIBBOUS TO WANING CRESCENT):

- Energy: Releasing, letting go, cleansing.

- Money Magic: This is a good time to release any limiting beliefs or negative thoughts surrounding money. It's also a powerful time for debt repayment rituals.

- Ritual Ideas: Perform a burning bay leaf ritual. Write down your limiting beliefs or debts on a bay leaf and burn it under the waning moon, visualizing them being released.

Something to think about: Moon magic is most effective when combined with practical financial planning and taking action. The lunar cycle provides an energetic framework to support your financial endeavors.

GRATITUDE EXERCISES FOR FINANCIAL ABUNDANCE:

Gratitude is a cornerstone of money magic. By appreciating what you already have, you open yourself up to receiving even more. Here are some powerful gratitude exercises to cultivate an abundant mindset:

1. THE DAILY ABUNDANCE JAR:

• Materials: A decorative jar, small pieces of paper.

• Instructions: Each day, write down at least 3 things you're grateful for related to your finances. This could be anything from a steady income to a surprise discount at the store. Fold the paper and place it in the jar. At the end of the week (or month), take some time to reread these notes and appreciate the abundance already present in your life.

2. THE FINANCIAL GRATITUDE LIST:

• Materials: A notebook or journal.

• Instructions: Dedicate a page or section of your journal to listing things you're grateful for financially. This could include:

+ A secure job you enjoy.

+ Savings that provide a safety net.

+The ability to afford basic needs.

+ Unexpected financial gifts or windfalls.

+ The knowledge and resources to manage your finances effectively. Review this list regularly and add new items as your financial situation evolves.

3. THE MONEY MAP:

• Materials: A large sheet of paper, colored pencils or markers, magazines (optional).

• Instructions: Create a visual representation of your financial goals. Draw a map of your ideal life, where money is not a source of stress. Include images from magazines or draw symbols that represent your financial desires (e.g., a dream house, a luxurious vacation, a car). Place this map somewhere you'll see it daily as a reminder of your gratitude for what you have and your excitement for what you're working towards.

4. THE "THANK YOU" NOTE TO ABUNDANCE:

- Materials: A piece of paper, a pen.

- Instructions: Write a heartfelt thank you note to the Universe, or a higher power you believe in, expressing your gratitude for the financial blessings in your life. Be specific about what you're grateful for and visualize these blessings multiplying. Fold the note and keep it in a special place, or burn it with the intention of releasing your gratitude into the Universe.

5. THE GRATITUDE MEDITATION:

- Instructions: Find a quiet space and get comfortable. Close your eyes and take a few deep breaths. Focus on your breath for a few minutes, calming your mind and body. Begin to visualize all the things you're grateful for in your life, especially those related to finances. Feel the emotions of gratitude wash over you. Spend 5-10 minutes basking in this feeling of appreciation. Slowly open your eyes, carrying the feeling of gratitude with you throughout the day.

These are just a few ideas to get you started. The key is to find gratitude practices that resonate with you and make them a regular part of your routine. By cultivating an attitude of gratitude, you'll be well on your way to attracting more abundance into your life.

PLAY WITH YOUR UNIVERSAL ABUNDANCE CHECK:

Here's your chance to get creative and train your mind for financial abundance! Imagine you're holding a blank check, a gift from the Universe, representing your limitless potential. Let's explore ways to interact with this check and solidify your belief in receiving wealth:

1 FILL IT OUT: Write in a specific amount you desire. Be bold! Don't limit yourself based on current circumstances.

2 DATE IT: CHOOSE a date in the near future, signifying your belief that this abundance is on its way.

3 ACCEPT IT AS "The Universe'Gift": This reinforces the idea that financial blessings are flowing to you from a limitless source.

4 VISUALIZE HOW YOU'LL Use It: Close your eyes and imagine the joy of receiving this money. How will you spend it? How will it improve your life?

5 WRITE A "THANK You" Note: Express gratitude to the Universe for its generosity and for your own deserving nature.

6 CARRY IT WITH You: Place the check in your wallet or purse. Seeing it regularly reminds you of your abundant mindset.

7 FRAME IT AND Display it: Hang it in a prominent place in your home or office as a daily affirmation of prosperity.

8 THINK ABOUT IT with Enthusiasm: Feel the energy of abundance flowing into your life.

9 WRITE A LIST of How You'll Earn It: Even with Universal abundance, co-creation plays a role. Brainstorm ways you can actively contribute to your financial goals.

10 USE IT FOR Inspiration: Look at the check when faced with financial limitations. It's a reminder that abundance is your birthright.

11 MEDITATE ON THE Feeling of Security: Close your eyes, hold the check, and visualize the peace of mind that comes with financial security.

12 REPLACE LIMITING BELIEFS: Every time you have a scarcity thought, look at the check and counter it with an affirmation of abundance (e.g., "There is always more than enough").

13 REPEAT! DO THIS exercise regularly. Repetition strengthens neural pathways associated with abundance and financial security. In the following pages you will find several checks for you to practice.

NOTE FROM THE AUTHOR:

Years ago, when I was just starting to explore the magic of money, I stumbled upon a "money check" exercise online. Inspired, I wrote myself a check for $16,000 and proudly displayed it next to my computer. Every time I sat down to work, I'd see the check and send a grateful message to the Universe. Weeks passed, and each time my eyes met the check, a small prayer of gratitude escaped my lips.

One day, a friend visited my office. We got to talking about selling books online, a business idea I'd been contemplating. To my surprise, my friend enthusiastically said, "Let's do it!" He then opened his suitcase and presented me with a check... for exactly $16,000!

Together, we launched our online book business, which continues to thrive after many years. But here's the funny thing: it took me a while to connect the dots! Believe it or not, the Universe's check still hung on my wall. Even though I'd received the very money I'd manifested, I kept expressing gratitude each time I saw it. It wasn't until a good three months later that it finally clicked - the money was already there! The miracle had unfolded, and I, in my blissful state of gratitude, hadn't even realized it!

So, my advice to you is: be mindful. Watch out for miracles. They happen, I can promise you. They do happen!!!!

Something to think about: this is a playful exercise to shift your mindset. Combine it with financial planning and taking action towards your goals to truly cultivate financial abundance.

Divine Providence
In Heaven   Date_____

PAY TO THE
ORDER OF:_____

_____
BANK
OF THE   *Divine Providence*
UNIVERSE

THIS MONEY
IS FOR: _____

_____

Divine Providence
In Heaven   Date_____

PAY TO THE
ORDER OF:_____

_____
BANK
OF THE   *Divine Providence*
UNIVERSE

THIS MONEY
IS FOR: _____

_____

| Divine Providence | |
| In Heaven | Date _____ |

PAY TO THE
ORDER OF: _____

BANK OF THE UNIVERSE *Divine Providence*

THIS MONEY
IS FOR: _____

| Divine Providence | |
| In Heaven | Date _____ |

PAY TO THE
ORDER OF: _____

BANK OF THE UNIVERSE *Divine Providence*

THIS MONEY
IS FOR: _____

Divine Providence
In Heaven   Date_____

PAY TO THE
ORDER OF: _____

_____

BANK
OF THE
UNIVERSE   **Divine Providence**

THIS MONEY
IS FOR: _____

_____

Divine Providence
In Heaven   Date_____

PAY TO THE
ORDER OF: _____

_____

BANK
OF THE
UNIVERSE   **Divine Providence**

THIS MONEY
IS FOR: _____

_____

Money Rituals

By Victoria Rey

Here's a list of 31 rituals, one for each day, that combine intention-setting with symbolic actions.

Here they are for you to practice the magic of money and to connect with its energy.

Make a different one for each and every day of the month, or...

Make one from the list every week, or

Repeat the same one everyday for a month.

Do what ever resonates with you.

In other words: Feel free to follow your instincts and your preferences. There are no rules here, for as long as you keep your words, thoughs and energy focused on being wealthy and having money flowing freely in your life, in a perfect, full of grace, and harmonious way.

DAILY MONEY RITUALS:

1	**GRATITUDE GLOW**	**NOTES:**
	LIGHT A GREEN CANDLE (abundance) and write down 3 things you're grateful for financially (even small wins). Focus on the warmth of the candle as gratitude fills you.	
2	**CLEAR THE COBWEBS**	**NOTES:**
	DECLUTTER YOUR WALLET AND bag. Throw away receipts and unused cards. Symbolically, remove obstacles to financial flow.	
3	**SEED OF PROSPERITY**	**NOTES:**
	PLANT A FAST-GROWING HERB (basil, mint) and visualize your finances flourishing alongside it. Water it daily with intention.	
4	**ABUNDANCE AFFIRMATION**	**NOTES:**
	LOOK IN THE MIRROR and repeat an affirmation like "I am a magnet for prosperity" 3 times. Believe the words as you say them.	
5	**COIN SHOWER**	**NOTES:**
	FIND A HEADS-UP PENNY outside. See it as a sign of coming abundance. Keep it in your wallet as a lucky charm.	

6	**DEBT DESTROYER**	**NOTES:**
	WRITE DOWN A MANAGEABLE debt amount. Light an orange candle (success) and visualize yourself burning through the debt with each flicker.	
7	**PROSPERITY BATH**	**NOTES:**
	ADD A FEW DROPS of cinnamon essential oil (wealth) to your bathwater. Relax and visualize financial security washing over you.	
8	**FULL MOON MONEY MAGIC**	**NOTES:**
	PLACE A BAY LEAF (prosperity) inscribed with "$" under moonlight. Charge it with your intention and keep it in your wallet.	
9	**CHARITABLE GIVING**	**NOTES:**
	DONATE A SMALL AMOUNT to a cause you care about. Karma has a way of returning generosity.	
10	**WINDFALL WISH**	**NOTES:**
	WRITE DOWN A SPECIFIC amount of money you desire for a purpose. Tie it to a green balloon and release it outside, sending your wish on the wind.	
11	**LUCKY PENNY JAR**	**NOTES:**
	EVERY TIME YOU FIND a heads-up penny, add it to a jar. Once full, donate the money to charity, expressing gratitude for your overflowing jar.	

12	**SPICE UP YOUR SAVINGS**	NOTES:
	ADD A CINNAMON STICK (wealth) to your piggy bank or coin jar.	
13	**BUDGET BLESSING**	NOTES:
	CREATE A REALISTIC BUDGET and visualize yourself sticking to it. See it as a tool for financial empowerment.	
14	**INVESTMENT INSPIRATION**	NOTES:
	RESEARCH A SMALL INVESTMENT you can make. Taking action shows the universe you're ready for abundance.	
15	**FREEBIE FINDER**	NOTES:
	LOOK FOR FREE OR discounted events, samples, or resources. Saving money is a form of gaining.	
16	**SKILLS FOR SALE**	NOTES:
	BRAINSTORM WAYS TO USE your skills to generate extra income.	
17	**INTERVIEW MAGIC**	NOTES:
	IF YOU HAVE A job interview, wear a green or gold piece of clothing (abundance, success).	
18	**RECEIPT RITUAL**	NOTES:
	WRITE "ABUNDANCE IS FLOWING" on a receipt from a recent purchase. Keep it in your wallet as a reminder.	

19	**DECLUTTER FOR DOLLARS**	**NOTES:**
	SELL UNWANTED ITEMS ONLINE or at a garage sale. Releasing clutter can make room for financial growth.	
20	**SUN SHOWER SAVINGS**	**NOTES:**
	PLACE A CLEAR JAR outside in the morning sunlight. As the day progresses, visualize your financial goals filling the jar with golden light. Bring it inside before sunset and keep it in a prominent place as a reminder.	
21	**DEBT DODGING DECLARATION**	**NOTES:**
	WRITE DOWN A LIST of all your debts. Next to each, write a clear plan for repayment (amounts, deadlines). Taking control fosters feelings of empowerment.	
22	**LUCKY NUMBER LOTTERY**	**NOTES:**
	PICK A NUMBER THAT resonates with you (birthday, lucky number) and visualize it bringing you financial luck. Play a small lottery or participate in a raffle (if legal in your area).	
23	**PROSPERITY POSTCARD**	**NOTES:**
	SEND A POSTCARD TO yourself with an image or message symbolizing abundance. Write a positive affirmation about your finances on the back.	

24	**WINDFALL WALK**	NOTES:
	TAKE A WALK IN nature and focus on feeling grounded and connected. Be open to finding unexpected money (coins, forgotten bills).	
25	**GRATITUDE GROVE (DAY**	NOTES:
	WRITE DOWN 5 THINGS you're grateful for financially on a piece of paper. Bury it under a healthy, thriving tree, visualizing your finances growing strong.	
26	**FRUGAL FEAST**	NOTES:
	PLAN A DELICIOUS AND affordable meal at home. Appreciate the savings and celebrate your budgeting skills.	
27	**INTERVIEW INSPIRATION**	NOTES:
	IF YOU HAVE AN upcoming interview, visualize yourself confidently answering questions and making a positive impression. See yourself receiving a job offer with the salary you desire.	
28	**BILL BUSTING BONFIRE**	NOTES:
	SAFELY BURN (FOLLOWING FIRE safety guidelines) any paid-off bills or receipts. Symbolically release the burden of debt and make space for new financial beginnings.	

29	**PROSPERITY PYRAMID**	NOTES:
	GATHER TEN COINS OF increasing value. Stack them in pyramid form, visualizing your wealth growing steadily.	
30	**NEW MOON NEW START**	NOTES:
	NEW MOON: UNDER THE new moon, write down a new financial goal. Light a white candle (new beginnings) and focus on the potential this new cycle brings.	
31	**Overflowing Offering**	NOTES:
	FILL A BOWL WITH rice or another grain (abundance symbol). Throughout the day, add a few grains each time you experience a bit of financial fortune (unexpected find, raise, etc.). Visualize your wealth overflowing.	

RAISING YOUR VIBRATION

UNDERSTANDING VIBRATION

In the context of the Law of Attraction, "vibration" refers to the frequency of energy that you emit based on your thoughts, feelings, and actions. Everything in the universe, including your thoughts and emotions, is made up of energy. This energy vibrates at different frequencies. High-frequency vibrations are associated with positive emotions like love, joy, gratitude, and peace, while low-frequency vibrations are linked to negative emotions such as fear, anger, sadness, and frustration.

WHY RAISING YOUR VIBRATION IS IMPORTANT:

ALIGNMENT WITH DESIRES:

When you raise your vibration, you align yourself with the higher frequencies of your desires. The Law of Attraction states that like attracts like. Therefore, by maintaining a high vibrational frequency, you attract experiences, people, and opportunities that resonate at that same frequency. For example, if you desire abundance, cultivating feelings of gratitude and joy can align your vibration with the energy of abundance.

ENHANCED MANIFESTATION POWER:

High vibrational states amplify your ability to manifest your desires more effectively and quickly. Positive emotions and thoughts create a powerful energy field that draws in the resources and circumstances needed to achieve your goals.

IMPROVED EMOTIONAL WELL-BEING:

Raising your vibration improves your overall emotional state. When you focus on positive thoughts and feelings, you naturally experience more happiness, contentment, and inner peace. This not only makes the manifestation process more enjoyable but also contributes to a healthier and more fulfilling life.

ATTRACTING POSITIVE RELATIONSHIPS:

High vibrations attract other high vibrational individuals. By raising your vibration, you naturally draw in people who are supportive, positive, and aligned with your values and goals. This can lead to more meaningful and fulfilling relationships both personally and professionally.

RESILIENCE AGAINST NEGATIVITY:

Maintaining a high vibration makes you more resilient to negative influences and situations. When your vibration is high, you are less likely to be affected by external negativity and more capable of maintaining a positive outlook, even in challenging circumstances.

HOW TO RAISE YOUR VIBRATION:

PRACTICE GRATITUDE:

Regularly acknowledging and appreciating the good in your life raises your vibration. Keeping a gratitude journal can help you focus on positive aspects and attract more of what you appreciate.

MEDITATE AND PRACTICE MINDFULNESS:

Meditation and mindfulness practices help you stay present and centered, reducing stress and increasing your overall sense of well-being.

ENGAGE IN POSITIVE ACTIVITIES:

Participate in activities that bring you joy and fulfillment, such as hobbies, exercise, spending time with loved ones, and being in nature.

AFFIRMATIONS AND POSITIVE THINKING:

Use positive affirmations to reinforce high vibrational thoughts and beliefs. Focus on what you want to attract, rather than what you lack.

SURROUND YOURSELF WITH POSITIVE ENERGY:

Spend time with positive people, listen to uplifting music, and create an environment that supports your high vibrational state.

By consciously raising your vibration, you align yourself with the energy of your desires, making the process of manifesting your dreams smoother and more effective. Remember, the higher your vibration, the more effortlessly you can attract what you truly want in life.

EXCERCISE

RAISE YOUR VIBRATION

Daydreaming about daily financial abundance from the Universe can be a powerful tool to cultivate an abundance mindset. Here's how you can craft your personal money-manifestation daydream:

SETTING THE SCENE:

Find a quiet, comfortable spot. Close your eyes and take a few deep breaths to relax and focus.

Imagine yourself waking up in a beautiful space that represents your ideal life. It could be your dream home, a luxurious hotel room, or anywhere that feels prosperous.

THE DAILY WINDFALL:

Notice a small, elegant box placed beside you. It's intricately wrapped in a rich, vibrant fabric.

As you open it, a gentle light spills out, revealing a note that reads, "A gift from the Universe to support your dreams."

Inside the box is a perfect amount of money, enough to cover your daily needs and a little extra. It could be cash, a check, or some other form that feels right to you.

FEELING THE ABUNDANCE:

Pick up the money and feel its texture in your hands. Sense the security and freedom it brings.

Visualize yourself using this money mindfully throughout the day. Perhaps you treat yourself to a delicious coffee, buy a small gift for someone you love, or put some aside towards a larger goal.

EXPANDING THE FEELING:

Imagine this happening every single day. The Universe consistently provides for you, allowing you to live comfortably and pursue your passions.

Feel the gratitude welling up inside you. Thank the Universe for its generosity and acknowledge your own deserving nature.

BRINGING THE DREAM BACK:

When you're ready, gently bring yourself back to the present moment. Take a deep breath and wiggle your fingers and toes.

Carry the feeling of abundance and gratitude with you throughout your day.

Remember:

This is your personal daydream. Feel free to personalize the details to resonate with you.

The key is to engage your senses and emotions to create a vivid and believable experience.

Practice this daydream regularly. Repetition strengthens the neural pathways associated with abundance and financial security.

While daydreaming isn't a guaranteed path to riches, it can be a powerful tool to shift your mindset and open yourself up to new possibilities. Combine it with financial planning and taking action towards your goals to truly cultivate financial abundance.

THE ANTIDOTE TO WORRY: A LESSON IN SPIRITUAL MARKETING

Let me tell you a story that transformed my perspective on wealth creation. Back in 2007, a friend recommended a book called "Spiritual Marketing" by Joe Vitale. It focused on creating abundance through a different lens.

In the book, Vitale recounts the tale of a friend facing a failing business. Wanting to help, Vitale confided in his own spiritual advisor. The advisor's response was a simple yet profound truth:

"He is worried about money because he is worried about money."

This resonated deeply with me. It highlighted the destructive nature of worry. When we fixate on financial anxieties, we drain our energy and limit our ability to take action.

Instead, the key lies in proactive solutions. We can create a plan, seek resources, communicate with creditors, and explore income generation strategies.

In essence, we use our words, thoughts, and energy to actively create wealth.

The message here isn't to ignore challenges. It's about shifting our focus. When we engage in constructive actions and cultivate a positive mindset, opportunities tend to emerge.

In simpler terms, when we focus on solutions, positive outcomes often follow naturally.

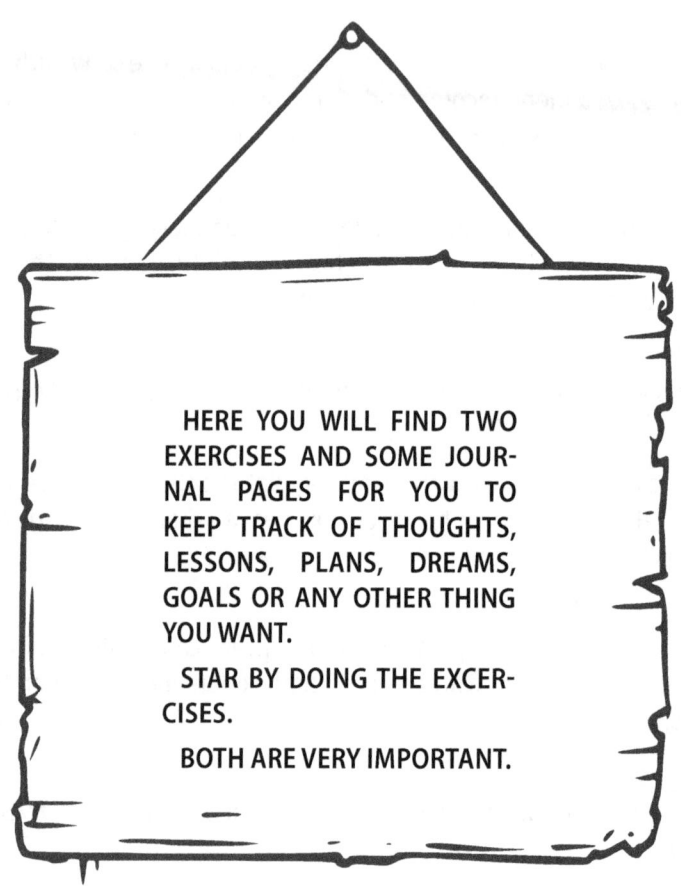

HERE YOU WILL FIND TWO EXERCISES AND SOME JOURNAL PAGES FOR YOU TO KEEP TRACK OF THOUGHTS, LESSONS, PLANS, DREAMS, GOALS OR ANY OTHER THING YOU WANT.

STAR BY DOING THE EXCERCISES.

BOTH ARE VERY IMPORTANT.

THINGS I DON'T WANT

Cut this page.

Write down the things you don't want in your life. For example: worry, debt collection calls, insomnia, insecurity, etc.

After you finish. Light a candle (refer to page 13th). In your mind, see these things "gone". Feel how they vanish from your life.

Then burn this list on the light of the candle.

SIGN HERE

DATE:_____

THINGS I WANT

Cut this page.

Write down the things you want in your life. For example: peace by living debt-free, money in my wallet, in my bank, a retirement account, a hourse, a car, healthy food in my fridge, etc.

After you finish. Light a candle (refer to page 13). Anoint the corners of your list. Bless it.

Save it in your wallet or put it in a place where you can see it frequently.

SIGN HERE

DATE: _____

Money Magic Journal

Here are some pages for you to keep track of your thoughts, learnings, inspiration, mantras, or anything you want to keep handy. On the right side top corner of some pages there is a blank square for you to put pictures or gratitudes or anything that brings you joy and inspiration.

BLESSINGS...

The knowledge and tools are now yours. Use them to claim your financial prosperity!

Remember, wealth is waiting for those who are prepared to receive it.

As you take action and cultivate the right mindset, witness the transformation in your life. The Universe is a place of abundance, and so are you.

This book has been your guide, but true wealth springs from a shift within yourself and a unwavering commitment to your goals.

May your journey be overflowing with abundance, not just material, but also in joy, purpose, and a life brimming with fulfillment.

Remember, the final act of magic lies in the belief you now hold close.

Weave your own spell of prosperity as you go forth.

The Universe is actively conspiring for your success.

Open yourself to the flow of abundance, and witness your dreams manifesting in magnificent ways.

Much love and ligh.

© All rights reserved. No part of this book may be reproduced in text or images by any means, without written permission.

© Calli Casa Editorial 2013
© Yhacar Trust, 2024

General Supervision: Bernabé Pérez.
www.2GoodLuck.com
Calli Casa Editorial
Lake Elsinore, CA 92530

www.ingramcontent.com/pod-product-compliance
Lightning Source LLC
LaVergne TN
LVHW051709080426
835511LV00017B/2804